Canadian Animals
Spirit Bears

Jennifer Howse

Weigl

Published by Weigl Educational Publishers Limited
6325 10th Street S.E.
T2H 2Z9

www.weigl.com
Canadian Animals series © 2011
Weigl Educational Publishers Limited

Library and Archives Canada Cataloguing in Publication

 Howse, Jennifer
            Spirit bears / Jennifer Howse.
(Canadian animals)
Includes index.
Issued also in electronic format.
ISBN 978-1-55388-662-4 (bound).–ISBN 978-1-55388-663-1 (pbk.)
1. Kermode bear–British Columbia–Juvenile literature.
I. Title. II. Series: Canadian animals (Calgary, Alta.)

QL737.C27H69

2010a   j599.78'509711   C2009-907370-6

Editor
Josh Skapin
Design
Terry Paulhus

Photograph Credits
Every reasonable effort has been made to trace ownership and to
obtain permission to reprint copyright material. The publishers would
be pleased to have any errors or omissions brought to their attention
so that they may be corrected in subsequent printings.

Weigl acknowledges Getty images as one of its primary image
suppliers for this title.
Peter Arnold: page 3, page 6, page 8, page 10, page 12, page 14,
page 15.

We gratefully acknowledge the financial support of the Government of
Canada through the Canada Book Fund for our publishing activities.

Printed in United States of America in North Mankato, Minnesota
1 2 3 4 5 6 7 8 9 0   14 13 12 11 10

072010
WEP230610

Contents

Meet the Spirit Bear

Spirit bears are a type of black bear that live in the **rain forests** of British Columbia. These black bears are rare. Unlike other black bears, spirit bears have white fur, with black skin underneath.

Spirit bears are also known as Kermode bears. They are named after scientist Francis Kermode. Kermode was one of the first people to study spirit bears.

▶ The spirit bear is sometimes called the ghost bear. This is because of its white fur.

Spirit Bear Facts

- Spirit bears have white fur, but they are not **albinos**.
- Spirit bear cubs from the same family may have black or white fur.

▲ Spirit bears can live up to 25 years in nature.

A Very Special Animal

Spirit bears are medium-sized bears. They are between 121 and 182 centimetres from the tip of their nose to the end of their tail. Spirit bears weigh between 68 and 136 kilograms. In comparison, grizzly bears weigh more than 363 kilograms.

▼ Spirit bears shed their fur each spring. Their new fur looks bright until it becomes dirty.

Spirit bears have small eyes.
These bears have good
vision and can see colours.

The spirit bear's
white fur is thick
and waterproof.
It keeps the bear
warm and dry.

These bears use
their claws to catch
fish or climb trees.

Where Do They Live?

Most spirit bears live on Princess Royal Island. Princess Royal Island is located within the Great Bear Rainforest. This is a region on the west coast of British Columbia. Here, 10 percent of black bears are born with white fur.

Spirit bears use trees as dens. They **hibernate** in these dens during winter. Spirit bears stay alert during hibernation. If they hear a noise, the bears will wake up to see if there is a threat.

▶ There are only about 400 spirit bears in British Columbia.

Spirit Bear Range

CANADA

British
Columbia

Alberta

Pacific
Ocean

Great Bear
Rainforest

UNITED
STATES

N
W — E
S

0
0
200 Kilometres

■ **Known Spirit Bear Range**

What Do They Eat?

Spirit bears are omnivores. This means they eat both meat and plants. Spirit bears eat nuts, fruits, roots, grasses, fish, plants, and even insects.

▼ Besides fish, spirit bears hunt deer and moose.

The spirit bear eats three to four meals a day. This can include two to three salmon at one time. The spirit bear fishes for salmon in the rain forest waters. It stands in a river and pins the fish with its front legs. Spirit bears then climb a tree before eating their **prey**. This is done so the bear's food is not stolen by a predator.

What a Meal!

Spirit bears go without food for up to seven months while hibernating. When preparing to hibernate, the spirit bear eats at least three times more food than it would in a normal day.

▲ Before hibernating, spirit bears sometimes spend 20 hours a day eating.

Living Alone

Most spirit bears prefer to live alone. Female bears live with their cubs until the cubs are ready to take care of themselves. This is one of the only times a spirit bear will live with other spirit bears.

▼ Mating season is the only other time spirit bears live together.

Spirit Bear Talk

Spirit bears use **scent markings** to leave messages for other bears. Frightened spirit bears chatter their teeth. Spirit bear cubs hum when they nurse or cuddle with their mother.

▲ Spirit bears communicate by grunting and clicking their tongue.

Growing Up

Female spirit bears can have babies of their own when they are three years old. They give birth to litters of one to three cubs at a time.

Mother bears help their cubs climb trees. Cubs wait for their mother in a tree until she finishes hunting. This keeps the cubs safe from predators.

▼ Cubs stay with their mother for up to two years.

► Mother spirit bears teach their cubs how to hunt.

Comparing Weights

Spirit Bear

At birth	225 grams
Adult female	70 kilograms
Adult male	135 kilograms

0 10 20 30 40 50 60 70 80 90 100 110 120 130 140 150 160 kilograms

Friends and Enemies

The spirit bear is a predator with few enemies in nature. Spirit bears will fight each other when defending their territory. They may also fight when trying to find a mate.

▼ Spirit bear cubs learn how to defend their territory at a young age.

Spirit bear cubs learn how to defend their territory by play fighting. Spirit bears sometimes play fight with their mother. She teaches them how to defend themselves.

◀ The average human male can run 20 kilometres an hour.

Comparing Speed

Spirit bears can run as fast as 55 kilometres per hour. This is nearly three times faster than most human males can run.

Under Threat

Spirit bears are **endangered** animals. Hunting spirit bears is against the law. Still, humans are a threat to spirit bears in other ways.

The **logging** industry is a major threat to spirit bears. A great deal of the spirit bear's **habitat** has been lost because of logging in British Columbia.

▼ More than half of the British Columbia's coastal rain forest has been logged.

▲ Some of the trees in the Great Bear Rainforest are more than 1,000 years old.

What Do You Think?

Do you believe parts of the rain forest where spirit bears live should be protected from logging? Should logging in the rain forest continue?

Myths and Legends

Spirit bears are a symbol of the rain forests in Canada. These bears represent fragile **ecosystems** only found in this country. Canadians have many stories about spirit bears.

First Nations tell how, at one time, the world was white. Raven decided he would make the world green. He kept spirit bears white to remind First Nations of the way the world was at the beginning of time.

▶ There are many First Nations legends about the raven.

The spirit bear is British Columbia's provincial animal. The spirit bear is also the official totem animal of British Columbia. Totems are important cultural symbols for First Nations of the northwest coast. A totem pole is a tall wooden carving that has shapes of animals and other creatures stacked one on top of the other. The meanings of totems are different between First Nations groups.

► Miga, a character who is part spirit bear, was one of the mascots at the 2010 Vancouver Olympics.

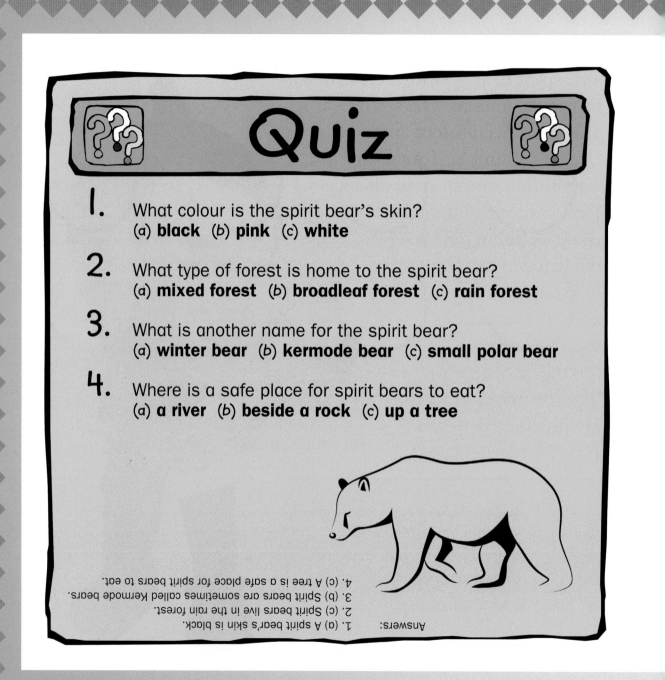

Quiz

1. What colour is the spirit bear's skin?
   (a) **black** (b) **pink** (c) **white**

2. What type of forest is home to the spirit bear?
   (a) **mixed forest** (b) **broadleaf forest** (c) **rain forest**

3. What is another name for the spirit bear?
   (a) **winter bear** (b) **kermode bear** (c) **small polar bear**

4. Where is a safe place for spirit bears to eat?
   (a) **a river** (b) **beside a rock** (c) **up a tree**

Answers:
1. (a) A spirit bear's skin is black.
2. (c) Spirit bears live in the rain forest.
3. (b) Spirit bears are sometimes called kermode bears.
4. (c) A tree is a safe place for spirit bears to eat.

Find out More

To find out more about spirit bears, write to the following organizations, or visit their websites.

Spirit Bear Youth Coalition
P.O. Box 91933
Vancouver, BC
V7V 4S4
www.spiritbearyouth.org

World Wildlife Fund, Canada
Suite 504
90 Eglinton Avenue East
Toronto, Ontario
M4P 2Z7
www.wwf.ca

Words to Know

albinos
people or animals that have no colour in their skin and hair

ecosystems
a community formed by living things in the environment

endangered
at risk of no longer living any place on Earth

habitat
the region where plants or animals grow or live

hibernate
to go into a deep sleep during winter

logging
cutting down trees in a forest

prey
an animal that is hunted for food

rain forests
forests in a tropical region that have an annual rainfall of at least 2.5 metres

scent markings
odours left on plants by animals rubbing against them

Index